YORK NOTES

Ethan Frome

Edith Wharton

Note by Tara Manuel-Rigler

Longman

York Press

Tara Manuel-Rogler is hereby identified as author of this work in accordance with Section 77 of the Copyright, Designs and Patents Act 1988

YORK PRESS
322 Old Brompton Road, London SW5 9JH

PEARSON EDUCATION LIMITED
Edinburgh Gate, Harlow,
Essex CM20 2JE, United Kingdom
Associated companies, branches and representatives throughout the world

First published 2000

ISBN 0–582–43179–4

Designed by Vicki Pacey
Phototypeset by Gem Graphics, Trenance, Mawgan Porth, Cornwall
Colour reproduction and film output by Spectrum Colour
Produced by Addison Wesley Longman China Limited, Hong Kong

Contents

Preface

York Notes are designed to give you a broader perspective on works of literature studied at GCSE and equivalent levels. We have carried out extensive research into the needs of the modern literature student prior to publishing this new edition. Our research showed that no existing series fully met students' requirements. Rather than present a single authoritative approach, we have provided alternative viewpoints, empowering students to reach their own interpretations of the text. York Notes provide a close examination of the work and include biographical and historical background, summaries, glossaries, analyses of characters, themes, structure and language, cultural connections and literary terms.

If you look at the Contents page you will see the structure for the series. However, there's no need to read from the beginning to the end as you would with a novel, play, poem or short story. Use the Notes in the way that suits you. Our aim is to help you with your understanding of the work, not to dictate how you should learn.

York Notes are written by English teachers and examiners, with an expert knowledge of the subject. They show you how to succeed in coursework and examination assignments, guiding you through the text and offering practical advice. Questions and comments will extend, test and reinforce your knowledge. Attractive colour design and illustrations improve clarity and understanding, making these Notes easy to use and handy for quick reference.

York Notes are ideal for:

- Essay writing
- Exam preparation
- Class discussion

The author of this Note, Tara Manuel-Rigler, is a writer, teacher and performing artist. She has an arts degree and is a graduate of the National Theatre School of Canada. In 1998 she was awarded the Fox Fellowship for excellence in the arts. She is currently at work on her second novel.

The text used in this Note is the Penguin Popular Classics edition, published in 1995.

***Health Warning:* This study guide will enhance your understanding, but should not replace the reading of the original text and/or study in class.**

INTRODUCTION

HOW TO STUDY A NOVEL

You have bought this book because you wanted to study a novel on your own. This may supplement classwork.

- You will need to read the novel several times. Start by reading it quickly for pleasure, then read it slowly and carefully. Further readings will generate new ideas and help you to memorise the details of the story.
- Make careful notes on themes, plot and characters of the novel. The plot will change some of the characters. Who changes?
- The novel may not present events chronologically. Does the novel you are reading begin at the beginning of the story or does it contain flashbacks and a muddled time sequence? Can you think why?
- How is the story told? Is it narrated by one of the characters or by an all-seeing ('omniscient') narrator?
- Does the same person tell the story all the way through? Or do we see the events through the minds and feelings of a number of different people.
- Which characters does the narrator like? Which characters do you like or dislike? Do your sympathies change during the course of the book? Why? When?
- Any piece of writing (including your notes and essays) is the result of thousands of choices. No book had to be written in just one way: the author could have chosen other words, other phrases, other characters, other events. How could the author of your novel have written the story differently? If events were recounted by a minor character how would this change the novel?

Studying on your own requires self-discipline and a carefully thought-out work plan in order to be effective. Good luck.

EDITH WHARTON'S BACKGROUND

Early life

Edith Newbold Jones was born in 1862 into a wealthy, distinguished family in New York. She never attended school, but was educated by governesses and foreign travel. This tightly controlled New York society positively discouraged women from achieving anything beyond a proper marriage. She 'came out' into society at a young age and in 1885, at the age of twenty-three, married a friend of her mother's, Edward Wharton, a man several years her senior.

In Edith Wharton's time women were not encouraged to have a career.

Influenced by the work of Henry James, a friend of her family and the author of such acclaimed novels as *The Americans* (1876), *The Portrait of a Lady* (1881) and *The Wings of the Dove* (1902), Edith Wharton decided to take up literary pursuits.

Later life and work

She began writing for *Scribner's Magazine* and published several short stories. Success came with her first full-length novel, *The Valley of Decision* (1902), a reconstruction of eighteenth-century Italy. Her next novel, *The House of Mirth* (1905), established Edith Wharton as a leading novelist of her time. Although noted for her sharp depiction of New York society during the early twentieth century, she spent ten years living and writing in New England, a setting that appears in two novels, a novella and fully a quarter of her short stories. In these works Edith Wharton turns from portraying the wealthy and elite to exploring enigmatic and poverty-stricken psyches and souls. The New England of these tales, which range from light comedy to horror, becomes a **metaphor** (see Literary Terms) for fierce poverty, cultural sterility and an oppressive Puritan heritage that both fascinated and repelled her.

The setting for Ethan Frome is inspired by the author's own experience of living in New England.

Europe

In 1907, Edith Wharton moved with her husband to France, where she remained until her death. She published *Ethan Frome* in 1911. It is set in the imaginary town of Starkfield, which the author places in the same county in New England in which she lived. The novel poignantly reflects the unhappy state of her own marriage. The couple separated after Edward Wharton suffered a nervous collapse, and they finally divorced in 1913. Edith Wharton settled in Paris where she continued her prolific writing career.

Edith Wharton expressed her own unhappiness through her work.

She became one of the few civilians during the First World War to be made a Chevalier of the Legion of Honour for her extensive humanitarian work in France. Her wartime experiences are reflected in works such as *Fighting France, from Dunkerque to Belfort* (1915), and *A Son at the Front* (1923).

In 1920, Edith Wharton published what is widely believed to be her masterpiece, *The Age of Innocence.* The novel deals with the familiar territory of New York society and manners, and was awarded the Pulitzer Prize for Fiction in 1921, making its author the first woman ever to receive that distinction.

She was awarded the Pulitzer Prize in 1921.

Despite having never gone to school or college, Edith Wharton became a prolific and celebrated writer, producing over forty books in forty years, including authoritative works on architecture, gardens and interior design. She was also the first woman to receive an honorary degree from Yale University.
Edith Wharton died in Paris in 1937.

CONTEXT & SETTING

The novel *Ethan Frome* is set in a small town in Massachusetts, called Starkfield. This is a fictitious town set in the same county in New England where, for ten years around the turn of the twentieth century, Edith Wharton made her home.

In the seventeenth century, Massachusetts was settled by thousands of Puritans, emigrating from all over England. The Puritans who settled there not only placed a distinctive stamp on New England, but were long to influence American life and thought.

Villages such as Starkfield began to be settled in the latter part of the seventeenth century.

Politics and the Church were closely intertwined, and men held the decision-making power. In the latter part of the seventeenth century, villages such as the imaginary Starkfield began to be settled.

Massachusetts had an extreme climate and stony soil, its main resources were timber and fish. This harsh yet beautiful land inspired Edith Wharton to set her novella in this place that she felt had been inaccurately represented in literature.

Turn-of-the-century New England

People abandoned farming districts for the cities.

Around the turn of the twentieth century, America was in the throes of its Industrial era. With the expansion of railroads, travel was made much easier. Many people left the land and went to live in the cities, attracted by the promise of a job in one of the many expanding industries. New England experienced the worst of the migration. Many people abandoned the once prosperous farming districts, and in the late nineteenth century the sight of abandoned and overgrown farms, tumble-down buildings and deserted villages became a common one.

During this time, American society was becoming increasingly polarised. In 1882, the Census Bureau estimated that 9 per cent of American families owned 71 per cent of the country's wealth. Thus despite the commonly held belief that America was a country that allowed almost anyone to achieve prosperity and security, there was little social mobility. For men like Ethan, this meant little opportunity for economic advancement.

Living conditions in the early twentieth century

During this period, a host of mechanical inventions and techniques transformed life and enriched the leisure hours of the common person. There were new methods of preserving foods, which meant a more varied and nutritious diet for many. The refrigerator was developed, making fresh meat available throughout the year. The refrigerator train car encouraged domestic fruit and vegetable growing, and with the rise of the ocean-going steamship, there was wider availability of tropical and subtropical fruit. The use of electric light was spreading rapidly, as well as that of the telephone. The first records were made and the Kodak camera became a mass obsession.

When the narrator introduces us to the town of Starkfield, we meet it at a time when the bicycle, the trolley and mail delivery were at such a standard as to increase communication between the scattered villages, and indeed the rest of the country. In the time of Ethan's youth, Starkfield was a far more isolated place, and information about the outside world was not easily accessed. There was no library, electricity, trolley, central heating or other such conveniences. There was no welfare system in place to help families like Ethan's who were tied to their land, barely able to survive. With this view in mind, it is easy to understand how Ethan's personality has been shaped by his circumstances.

Starkfield was isolated, having few modern conveniences.

The late eighteenth century witnessed a great advance in American literature. There was a movement toward literary **realism** (see Literary Terms). Finding their subject matter in the customs and dialect of their own regions, writers generally concentrated on a vanishing rural past. Edith Wharton was among this group of well-known writers.

Many artists criticised this era, insisting it was characterised by a materialism and vulgarity that were destructive to intellectual and artistic life and work. Success in business was valued above intellectual or artistic achievement. America produced little of value in music or drama and continued to look to Europe for inspiration in architecture, sculpture and painting. It is little wonder that so many writers and painters felt compelled to leave America for Europe. Edith Wharton, of course, was among them.

Many artists moved to Europe.

The role of women in the early twentieth century

During this period, women's independence was growing. New legislation enlarged married women's property rights, gave them control over their earnings and property, and gave them the right to make contracts without their husband's consent. Industrialisation provided them with better opportunities for supporting themselves. While most of the jobs available to women were low paid, work provided them with an independence that they had not known before. More employment opportunities and the spread of women's higher education brought an increase in the age at which they generally married, and in the number of women remaining unmarried. Divorce rates increased, with two-thirds of divorce suits being filed by women. Despite these advances, women were still not granted the right to vote.

Women were beginning to gain some independence.

Examination boards increasingly insist that you study a novel within its historical context. Consider how much *Ethan Frome* is affected by the times in which the author lived, and how much it is a novel about those times.

PART TWO

SUMMARIES

GENERAL SUMMARY

(Untitled) introduction – Chapter 2: Meeting Ethan Frome

We are introduced to the story by the narrator, who remains nameless. The narrator is intrigued by the mystery surrounding Ethan and hires the lame and seemingly aged man to drive him to and from his work at Corbury Flats for one week. We discover that despite his appearance, Ethan is only fifty-two, and his scarred face and shortened right side are the result of a mysterious 'smash-up' that occurred twenty-four years before. The story of Ethan's tragic life now begins with the young Ethan on a clear winter night, walking through deserted streets to the church where he meets his wife's cousin, Mattie Silver, to accompany her home. We learn that Mattie has lived with Ethan for one year, and that he enjoys very much to be in her company. When they arrive at the farm, the door is locked and they are surprised by Zeena, Ethan's wife, who opens it, looking rather like a ghost. Zeena, as usual, complains about her health and beckons Ethan to bed. Reluctantly he follows, and they all retire for the night.

Chapters 3–5: Understanding relationships

The next day is clear and still, and finds Ethan up early, hauling wood from his saw mill. He cannot help thinking of Mattie, and chides himself for not kissing her the night before. We learn of Mattie's sad life, and of how her health has improved since coming to Starkfield. Zeena decides to spend the night with her aunt in Bettsbridge as she wishes to consult a doctor there, and Ethan delights at the prospect of spending an evening alone with Mattie. We learn that Zeena nursed Ethan's mother and that he felt compelled to marry her. Ethan muses over how Zeena has grown ever more silent and miserable and we understand that Mattie fulfils him in a way Zeena never could. Ethan asks Mr Hale, a builder, for an advance of fifty dollars, and is refused. He returns to find that Mattie has prepared his supper. One of Zeena's precious dishes is broken and Ethan comforts Mattie, saying he will mend it and Zeena need never know. They spend a quiet evening together.

Chapters 6–8: Heading for disaster

The next day, Ethan has a difficult time on the farm, and later than anticipated, heads into town to buy glue to mend Zeena's dish. When he returns home he is dismayed to discover that Zeena has arrived earlier than expected. He finds her in their bedroom, sitting rigidly. Zeena tells him that the doctor has strongly advised her to hire a girl as she is no longer capable of lifting a finger to work. She reveals, much to Ethan's dismay, that she has hired a new girl who will arrive the following day, and that Mattie must leave. Ethan goes to Mattie and as he tells her the news he kisses her for the first time. Zeena comes down to join them for dinner and discovers her broken dish. She lashes out at Mattie and retires to her room. Ethan spends the night in his study and, after hours of deliberating, decides to run away with Mattie. He soon realises the impossibility of this as he lacks the funds, and the next morning makes his way to Mr Hale's farm to borrow money under the pretence of needing to buy Zeena some medication. On the way he meets Mrs Hale, and cannot bring himself to lie about his circumstances. He turns towards home.

Chapter 9–(Untitled) epilogue: The mystery revealed

When Ethan returns to the farm, he finds Mattie weeping in her room. He insists upon driving her to the Junction himself. He takes the long way there as he strives to enjoy his last hour with her. They reminisce over times spent together in the places they pass and Mattie reveals a note that Ethan had written to Zeena to say goodbye. The note describes the plan he was unable to put into action. They speak, for the first time, of their feelings for one another. As they draw near the hill with the slide by the church, they decide to toboggan down together one last time. They ascend the hill and embrace, unable to face that Mattie is to leave. They decide to slide down again, making sure they hit the great elm at the bottom, and die together, rather than be parted. They do not die; instead both are crippled for life. The story now returns to the present where the narrator is discovered in Ethan Frome's kitchen, and we see Mattie, a cripple, and Zeena, an old woman, sitting in a cold bare room. The narrator returns to his lodgings at Mrs Hale's house. She reveals her belief that Mattie and Ethan would have been better off had they died on that fateful night.

DETAILED SUMMARIES

(UNTITLED) INTRODUCTION

Notice how the fact that Ethan is prematurely old and has a scar whets our curiosity.

The novel opens with the unnamed narrator describing the first time he saw Ethan Frome. The sight of the disfigured man was quite a shock. The narrator is surprised to hear from a local named Harmon Gow that Ethan is only fifty-two, as he is stiff and grey like an old man. Harmon reveals that the red gash across Ethan's forehead and his lame right side are the result of a mysterious 'smash-up' which occurred twenty-four years before. Ethan drives into town every day, often to pick up medicine for his sickly wife. The narrator says that Ethan looks as if he were already dead and in hell.

Ethan has spent his life caring first for his father, then mother and now his wife. The narrator is curious to discover more about Ethan, and as he is in need of a ride to his work in Corbury Flats and Ethan is in need

The narrator is hoping to get to know Ethan, but he is silent.

of money, he hires Ethan to drive him to and fro for one week. They pass their time together in almost complete silence. During the last trip of the week, a fierce storm blows up, making any further progress impossible. Ethan offers the narrator shelter for the night at his farm and the narrator tells us that this night he began to piece together the story of Ethan Frome.

COMMENT

Before the tale of Ethan Frome actually begins, we are introduced to the story by the narrator. This device is known as a **frame narrative** (see Literary Terms).

We learn some facts about Ethan. First, and most obviously, we learn his scarred face and shortened right side are due to a 'smash-up' that occurred twenty-four years before. We learn that Ethan is a quiet, private man by nature, and that he has spent his life caring for his ailing family.

Ethan's personality reflects the landscape he was brought up in.

We learn something of the land in which this story is set and of how it is reflected in Ethan's character. The landscape is described as being melancholy, and Ethan as a representation of its 'frozen woe' (p. 11).

Note the **images** (see Literary Terms) such as trees bending inward, and the Frome's diminished house, and how they reflect Ethan's shrunken physique. Note also the **metaphor** (see Literary Terms) comparing the advance of winter to an army: 'the storms … had pitched their white tents … the wild cavalry of March winds'.

Note how often death is referred to in this introduction. It is one of the main **themes** (see Literary Terms and Themes) running throughout the novel.

GLOSSARY

bay dark reddish-brown horse
pulled me up sharp startled me
grizzled having grey hair

pre-trolley days days before trolley-buses
buggy two-wheeled horse-drawn vehicle
specific particular medicine or remedy
Carcel lamp light working on paraffin which is pumped by clockwork
livery stable stable with horses for hire
hemlock a type of conifer
exanimate lacking life
pike toll-gate

CHAPTER 1

The story now begins, twenty-four years before, with the young Ethan Frome walking alone on a clear winter night. We learn that Ethan spent a year at a technical college before having to give up his studies of physics to care for his ailing parents. His studies, although of no practical use, served to enrich his sensitive nature. Ethan arrives at the church and peers in the windows at revellers enjoying the last dance of the evening. One girl in particular attracts his attention. She is Mattie Silver, his wife's cousin, whom he has come to accompany on the two-mile walk back to his farm. We learn that Mattie came to live with Ethan one year before and that Ethan has romantic feelings for her. He reflects on how his wife Zeena, a miserable hypochondriac, has hinted at her displeasure with Mattie's housework skills. We understand that Ethan's relationship with his wife is an unhappy one and that Zeena has grown bitter over the years. Ethan watches with jealousy as Mattie dances a reel with a young man named Denis Eady.

The fact that Ethan is married may mean that his romantic feelings are already doomed.

COMMENT

In this chapter we learn of Ethan's love of nature, and how his brief studies have given a form to this passion, so that, even in his unhappiest moments, he is able to find solace in nature. We learn of Ethan's delight to find in Mattie someone who could share in these passions, and with whom he can feel smart and capable (see Part Three, on Character).

MEETING ETHAN FROME

This chapter begins Ethan's struggle with feeling trapped in his unhappy marriage with Zeena and his overwhelming love for Mattie.

We take an immediate dislike of Zeena. Note the words the author uses to describe this character: 'sickly', 'her queer looks' (p. 27), 'her flat whine' (p. 28) Note also Ethan's fear of his wife.

GLOSSARY

the Dipper, Orion, Adelbaran, the Pleiades stars and constellations

exhausted receiver a term from eighteenth-century physics referring to a bell-jar used to create a vacuum

coasting-ground toboggan slide

fascinator head scarf

suspenders braces

CHAPTER 2

Ethan waits, unseen, as the dancers pour out of the church hall. He watches as Denis Eady tries to convince Mattie to allow him to drive her home. Ethan is elated when she refuses his offer and begins the long walk by herself. Ethan catches up with her, and they link arms, delighting in this time together. Ethan promises that he will take Mattie 'sliding' (tobogganning) the following evening. He hints that Mattie would be interested in marrying and leaving the

Think whether it is likely that Ethan can keep his promise.

farm. Mattie replies tearfully that she has nowhere else to go, and we understand that she has no interest in leaving Ethan's home. For the first time, Ethan wraps his arms around her. When they arrive at the farm, the door is locked. Zeena opens it to them, and when Ethan sees her he feels as if he is really seeing her for the first time. She looks thin and gaunt and, as usual, complains about her health. She beckons Ethan to bed and reluctantly he follows.

COMMENT

Note Ethan's shyness and his difficulty with expressing himself. As he searches for something exciting to say, all he can think of is, 'Come along' (p. 34). This contrasts with the author's use of poetic description. She compares the sliding hill to a mirror that has been scratched by travellers at an inn.

Notice the author's use of **metaphor** (see Literary Terms) in describing Mattie. She compares the motions of Mattie's mind to that of the unpredictable and erratic movements of a bird in a tree.

Consider whether Ethan is acting rationally here.

In this chapter Ethan becomes jealous when Denis Eady offers Mattie a ride. Even after she refuses him and she and Ethan have begun their walk toward home, Ethan cannot let his jealousy go.

It is interesting that one of Ethan's happiest visions is of he and Mattie being buried together in the Frome graveyard.

Observe the author's use of light in describing Zeena. When Ethan looks at her in this light he feels as if he is seeing her for the first time (see Language & Style).

GLOSSARY

cutter horse-driven sleigh
arch coyly playful
rapture joyous ecstasy
crimping-pins hair curlers

Test yourself (Introduction–Chapter 2)

A *Identify the speaker.*

1 'He's looked that way ever since he had his smash-up; and that's twenty-four years ago come next February'

2 '*That* man touch a hundred? He looks as if he was dead and in hell now!'

3 'I guess you're always late, now you shave every morning'

4 'No, I wouldn't be mean enough to tell the other girls. I ain't as low-down as that'

5 'Oh Ned ain't much at steering. I guess I can take you down all right!'

Identify the person(s) 'to whom' this comment refers.

6 'He seemed a part of the mute melancholy landscape'

7 'She don't look much on housework, but she ain't a fretter, anyhow'

8 'You know she hardly ever says anything, and sometimes I can see she ain't suited, and yet I don't know why'

Check your answers on page 67.

B *Consider these issues.*

- **a** The inevitability of the novel's end helps build suspense and makes Ethan Frome more tragic.
- **b** Why Ethan never continued his studies.
- **c** Why Ethan finds the idea of Mattie being buried next to him a comforting one.
- **d** Why Ethan and Zeena don't have children.
- **e** How much of an impact the land has had on the development of Ethan's character.

CHAPTER 3

The next morning dawns clear and still, and finds Ethan out early, hauling wood. Ethan reflects on the previous evening and chides himself for not kissing Mattie while he had the chance. He muses over how Mattie's health has improved since coming to Starkfield, after her father died leaving her virtually penniless. He worries about Zeena's silence since the previous evening and dreads having to see her. When he returns to the house, he is delighted to find that Zeena has made plans to stay overnight with her aunt in Bettsbridge as she wishes to consult a doctor there. He tells Zeena that he is unable to drive her to the train station as he must visit Mr Hale in order to collect some cash he owes Ethan for lumber, which is untrue. He immediately regrets this lie and realises his mistake in allowing Zeena to think there was money to spend when she was going on an excursion.

Through lying Ethan has embroiled himself in problems.

COMMENT

Note the author's use of colour in the second paragraph. The sunrise 'burned red' in the sky, the shadows near the wood-lot were 'darkly blue', and the fields were 'white and scintillating' (p. 42). This language is vivid and compelling and allows us to visualise easily the setting.

In this chapter we see Ethan and Zeena in a rare private moment. As Ethan reflects on the events of the previous evening, he reveals that not a word passed between them when they were alone in their room, and that he undressed quickly and blew out the light so that he would not have to see her. As he lies in bed with Zeena, all he can think of is Mattie. This marriage is obviously an unhappy one.

Consider whether it is possible to feel sympathy for Zeena.

In this chapter we learn of many of Zeena's unpleasant qualities. We learn that her fault-finding, though silent, is very disturbing. She devotes a great deal of her time to her various ailments. Much of her time is given to overspending Ethan's money on medicines and doctors, so much so that he has grown to dread her medical consultations because of their cost (see Part Three, on Characters).

Ethan so much desires to spend time alone with Mattie that he makes the mistake of lying to Zeena. From what we have discovered thus far, this is out of character for Ethan.

GLOSSARY

scintillating sparkling
slip of a thing thin and small
indentured bound as an apprentice or servant
'Curfew shall ... to-night', 'The Lost Chord' sentimental nineteenth-century poem and song
merino a type of wool
valise suitcase
sorrel light reddish-brown horse

CHAPTER 4

There seems to be no-one of similar intellect to whom Ethan could talk.

When Zeena leaves, Ethan bids Mattie goodbye and departs for the village with a load of wood. As he drives, he reflects on how his home is improved by the absence of his wife. He imagines how he and Mattie will spend their evening alone together. We are told that despite Ethan's quiet nature, he enjoyed interacting with the fellows at Worcester, where he studied, and how since returning to Starkfield his life has been spent in almost complete silence. We learn how his mother grew silent in the years before her death, and that when his cousin Zeena came to nurse her, just the sound of another person's voice made Ethan feel alive again. Ethan admits that it was his fear of silence that inspired him to ask Zeena to stay and marry him, rather than love. Ethan wonders if Zeena's growing silence is a sign that she is turning 'queer' in the way his mother did.

Ethan arrives at Mr Hale's with his lumber and his request for an advance of fifty dollars is refused. He

Think whether Ethan can hide the broken dish from someone as sharp-eyed as Zeena.

returns to the farm to find Mattie waiting for him with his supper ready, and happily they sit down to eat. Zeena's special glass dish is broken by the cat, and Mattie becomes terribly upset. Ethan comforts her that he will fix the dish and that Zeena need never know. Ethan plans to buy some glue and repair the dish the following morning.

COMMENT

Note the author's use of light in the first page of this chapter. She describes the kitchen as being bright and warm. She traces the sunlight through the window, on to Mattie, to the cat, to the geraniums. On his way into the village, Ethan reflects on how 'homelike' the kitchen seemed to him this morning as he bid Mattie goodbye. He attributes this warmth to the fact that Zeena is away (see Language & Style).

In this chapter we learn what compelled Ethan to marry Zeena. After the death of his mother he could not bear the thought of being alone on the farm, so he asked Zeena to stay. It is very sad when the author reveals that Ethan had often thought that if his mother had died in spring instead of winter, he would never have asked Zeena to marry him.

We learn that Zeena prevented Ethan from fulfilling his potential. It is revealed that Ethan had dreams of a successful future, that he had wanted to be an engineer, and to live a big town where he could have access to libraries, information and stimulating people. He soon realised, once Zeena developed her sickliness, that it would be impossible to go anywhere, and gave up the idea of leaving the farm.

Consider whether it is the harsh life and lack of hope that make Zeena silent.

Ethan fears Zeena's growing silence. He wonders if, like his mother, she is turning 'queer'. He refers to other women in the neighbourhood whose life was tragic, and when he looks at Zeena's face, he worries that fate has something similar in store for her. Here the author uses the device of **foreshadowing** (see Literary Terms) to alert us to the impending **tragedy** (see Literary Terms).

Ethan's pride is revealed when he will not admit to Mr Hale that he is in need of money.

Zeena's glass dish breaking foreshadows the shattering of the characters' lives. The dish is a **symbol** (see Literary Terms) of Ethan and Mattie's fragile happiness and indeed also of their health.

GLOSSARY

spruce neat, smart and trim
pathological relating to, involving, or caused by disease
cupolo cupola – a round dome, implying extravagance
in a tight place in a difficult situation
spangled made to glitter or shine

CHAPTER 5

The fact that this will be their only evening together makes the episode more poignant.

Ethan and Mattie finish supper then sit together. Mattie sews while Ethan smokes his pipe. Ethan beckons her to sit closer so that he may see her. Mattie sits in Zeena's rocking chair and for a moment Ethan thinks he sees his wife's face rather than Mattie's. Mattie becomes uncomfortable and changes seats. They chat amiably and Ethan promises Mattie that if there is a moon on the following evening, he will take her sliding. They refer openly, for the first time, to Zeena's ungracious attitude toward Mattie. Ethan silently laments the passing of this evening. He clasps and kisses the cloth Mattie sews. She rises to prepare for bed and as they bid one another goodnight, Ethan remembers that he has not even touched her hand.

COMMENT

Longing is one of the main themes in the novel. In this chapter Ethan and Mattie spend their only evening alone together. Ethan struggles with his desire for Mattie and his knowledge that his feelings for her are inappropriate, as he is married to Zeena. When he touches the cloth that Mattie sews it is as if he is touching Mattie herself, and when on an impulse he kisses the cloth in her hands, it is as if he kisses her. This is the most demonstrative of his feelings for Mattie that Ethan has been so far (see Themes).

Zeena's overpowering presence is felt even in her absence.

In this chapter, Zeena's presence is strongly felt. Mattie cannot find comfort in sitting in Zeena's chair, and for a moment Ethan thinks he sees the face of his wife instead of Mattie's. When they speak her name out loud it seems to echo in the room.

Much of Ethan and Mattie's communication takes place in silence. They are so attuned to one another that even the subtlest movement becomes an important means of communication.

GLOSSARY

muffled wrapped up

TEST YOURSELF (CHAPTERS 3–5)

A Identify the speaker.

1 'It ain't done me a speck of good, but I guess I might as well use it up'

2 'See here – you ain't in a tight place, are you?'

3 'She needn't know anything about it if you keep quiet. I'll get another just like it to-morrow'

4 'I ain't any more scared than you are!'

5 'That's an ugly corner down by the big elm. If a fellow didn't keep his eyes open he'd go plumb into it'

Identify the person(s) 'to whom' this comment refers.

6 'He came in after he got back, and asked for a drop of coffee before he went down home'

7 'Yes, but, you see, she never meant it should be used, not even when there was company'

8 'Say Matt, what do you think I saw under the Varnum spruces, coming along home just now? I saw a friend of yours getting kissed'

Check your answers on page 67.

B Consider these issues.

a How the author makes Zeena a disagreeable character.

b Why Ethan does not leave Zeena.

c Mattie's tenuous position in the household.

d Why Ethan does not tell Mattie he loves her.

e How the author often describes Zeena as having ghost-like qualities.

HEADING FOR DISASTER

CHAPTER 6

The next morning, they are joined for breakfast by Jotham Powell, a man who occasionally works for Ethan. Ethan tries to hide his happiness as he muses over the evening spent with Mattie. On the way to the wood-lot, one of the horses slips and is wounded. Ethan worries about having enough time to get into the village to buy glue and mend Zeena's dish before Jotham arrives with her at the farm. After dinner he rushes into town and back and is dismayed to discover that Zeena has arrived before him. Ethan wonders why Jotham refuses his invitation of a meal, and intuits that Zeena has taken out her frustrations on the man. He enters the kitchen where Mattie has laid the supper and they regard one another silently.

Consider the consequences when Ethan does not have time to glue Zeena's dish.

COMMENT

Other than moments spent in the presence of Mattie, Ethan's only happy ones are those he lives in fantasy. In this chapter he reflects on his evening with Mattie and how it had given him a vision of how their life together might be. Ethan is glad that he did nothing to spoil the sweetness of his fantasy.

This chapter signals the end of the relative peace in the household. Ethan's plan to glue Zeena's dish before she arrives is thwarted by the weather and by his horse's injury. He sets out for town much later than expected to fetch some glue, and when he returns Zeena has already arrived.

Consider how different the story would have been, had Ethan glued back Zeena's dish.

Jotham Powell's rejection of Ethan's offer to stay to dinner signals to Ethan that Zeena is in a bad mood. Ethan dreads seeing his wife.

When Ethan enters the kitchen the lamplight shines on the same scene of comfort as the night before. Yet the **atmosphere** (see Literary Terms) in the house has changed since Zeena's return.

GLOSSARY

milden grow mild
teaming working together

traveller's joy a wild climbing plant found in hedgerows
worked like ten worked hard and fast
anything she sets store by anything very important to her

CHAPTER 7

In this chapter disaster follows disaster, with Zeena's discovery of the broken dish being the final straw.

Ethan goes upstairs to greet his wife and to ask whether she is coming down to supper. As usual she refuses, and tells him that she is a great deal sicker than he thinks. Zeena tells him that the doctor said she shouldn't do anything around the house, and that she should hire a girl to help. She then tells Ethan that she has already hired someone who will arrive the next day. Ethan is terribly upset by this news and no longer believes that Zeena is sick. They argue over how Ethan is supposed to pay for the hired girl. It is the first openly angry argument between them. Zeena catches Ethan in his lie about having to see Mr Hale instead of driving her to the train. She then tells him that Mattie must leave. They argue again. Ethan feels hatred for his wife. He leaves the room and goes to the kitchen where Mattie serves him his meal. He is unable to eat and when Mattie questions him, he kisses her for the first time. Mattie then makes Ethan tell her what Zeena has decided. They are both upset. Zeena enters the room, behaving as if everything is as usual until she discovers her broken dish. Mattie tells her straight away that she got the dish down because she wanted the supper table to look pretty, and Zeena lashes out at her, calling her a bad girl. Zeena leaves the room, carrying the dish as if it were a dead body.

COMMENT

Zeena reveals to Ethan that she has 'complications'. We learn that almost everyone in Starkfield has 'troubles' with their health, yet only the chosen few have 'complications'. It seems as though people in Starkfield gain status through illness, and that Zeena strives for the highest distinction.

The first openly angry argument between Ethan and Zeena occurs. This signals the breaking of the façade of their marriage. Ethan becomes aware for the first time of the extent of Zeena's manipulation. He no longer believes that she is ill, and sees in her going to Bettsbridge a conspiracy between her relatives and herself to force upon him the cost of a servant.

Zeena gives her only obvious indication that she knows how Ethan feels about Mattie. She alludes to what people say about Mattie having stayed with them for so long.

Ethan cannot bring himself to strike his wife.

Zeena makes Ethan so angry that he is tempted to hit her. For a moment such hatred rises in him that he raises his fist against her. Yet he stops short of hitting her. Ethan cannot bring himself knowingly to hurt another person.

Mattie's strength of character is revealed. When Ethan blurts out the news that she must leave, instead of feeling sorry for herself, Mattie comforts Ethan. She tells him not to worry about her. When Zeena accuses Ethan of breaking her dish, Mattie stands up for him and readily admits her part in the accident.

GLOSSARY

dragging down-at-the-heel step shuffling; walking without picking up the feet

mite bit

CHAPTER 8

We are told that, when Ethan was forced to quit his studies and return to the farm to care for his father, his mother gave him a room for his use that he turned into a kind of study. He retreats to this cold room after finding a note left for him by Mattie telling him not to worry. He contemplates leaving his miserable wife and running away with Mattie and even goes as far as to write Zeena a farewell note. He soon realises that his dire financial situation offers him no way out and thinks of himself as a prisoner. He sleeps in the study. When he wakes Mattie discovers him in the room, and they go together into the kitchen. Ethan deludes himself for a moment that Zeena will change her mind, yet he is helpless to do anything to change his wife's arrangements. In a last attempt to find a way out of the situation, Ethan heads into town, planning to ask Mr Hale for an advance of money under the pretext of Zeena needing medication. On the way he meets Mrs Hale who expresses her sympathy for him. Ethan cannot bring himself to take advantage of the Hales' sympathy, and heads for home.

Think about the reasons why Ethan cannot leave Zeena.

COMMENT

In an effort to find happiness with Mattie, Ethan decides to leave Zeena and the farm. When he is writing his farewell note, he realises that he has no money, and no possibility of obtaining any, and he sees the futility of his situation. Money is one of the major themes in the novel (see Themes). Ethan's circumstances would be very different had he even a little.

Note the **simile** (see Literary Terms) the author uses when Ethan realises he has no money. The facts of his poverty are compared to prison warders, and Ethan a convict being handcuffed. Ethan feels himself a prisoner in his life with Zeena.

In one of Ethan's lowest moments, the author uses some of her most beautiful description. When Ethan looks out at slopes 'bathed in lustre' and 'the spectral purple of the hills against the sky', it seems to him that all the beauties of the night have been 'poured out to mock his wretchedness' (p. 99). This serves to contrast Ethan's dreary reality with the profound beauty of his surroundings.

GLOSSARY

lumbago type of backache
set ... the fire sit very close to the fire

TEST YOURSELF (CHAPTERS 6–8)

A *Identify the speaker.*

1 'Looks as if we were all sold out. But if you'll wait around till the old man comes along maybe he can put his hand on it'

2 'I'm obliged to you, but I guess I'll go along back'

3 'I didn't need to have anybody to tell me I was losing ground every day. Everybody but you could see it'

4 'But this new doctor has scared her about herself. You know she believes all they say the first time she sees them'

5 'You've had an awful mean time, Ethan Frome'

Identify the person(s) 'to whom' this comment refers.

6 'She's a pauper that's hung onto us all after her father'd done his best to ruin us'

7 'He woke up with a touch o' lumbago, and I just made him put on one of old Dr. Kidder's plasters and set right up to the fire'

8 'I'm real sorry she's feeling so bad again! I hope he thinks he can do something for her'

Check your answers on page 67.

B *Consider these issues.*

a Why Ethan fantasises so often.

b The human need for love and understanding.

c Why Ethan fears his wife.

d How the writer builds tension in this section.

e Why the glass dish is so important to Zeena.

f Why Ethan and Zeena have never argued before.

g Why Ethan does not stand up to Zeena and demand that Mattie stay.

CHAPTER 9

When Ethan arrives at the house he finds Daniel Byrne, the man whom Zeena has arranged to take Mattie to the station, waiting outside in his sleigh.

He finds Mattie upstairs in her room weeping. Ethan comforts her, then, despite Zeena's wishes, decides to take her to the station himself. Zeena does not even bid Mattie goodbye. Ethan and Mattie begin their journey, taking the long way round and reminiscing over times spent together in the places they pass. They stop at Shadow Pond and remember an afternoon spent together at a picnic. They begin on their way again, discussing what Mattie is to do in Stamford. Mattie reveals the note that Ethan had begun to write to Zeena the previous evening. Ethan demands to know, if it had been possible, whether Mattie would have gone with him. They speak openly for the first time of their feelings for one another. As they draw near the hill by the church, Ethan has the sudden impulse to slide down with Mattie. They find a sled nearby and coast down. They walk back up the hill and despair of having to leave one another. Mattie asks Ethan to take her down again, this time ensuring that they smash into the great elm near the bottom and die, so that they will never have to leave one another. Ethan complies, they kiss, and glide down the hill on the sledge, colliding

Only now, when they are to part, do Ethan and Mattie reveal their true feelings for one another.

Consider why Ethan goes along with Mattie's plan.

with the tree. The chapter ends with the two unable to move, yet still alive.

COMMENT

Ethan stands up to Zeena for the first time. Despite Zeena's wishes, he insists upon driving Mattie to the station himself. Ethan does not seem to want to face what is happening and when he and Mattie begin the drive, he behaves as if they are merely taking a ride for pleasure. When they reveal openly their fondness for one another, Ethan imagines that he is a single man, wooing the girl he would like to marry. Ethan retreats into a fantasy world instead of taking action to change his situation.

It is **ironic** (see Literary Terms) that only now when they are to part can Ethan and Mattie admit their love for one another.

In this chapter the tension builds to a terrible **climax** (see Literary Terms). The novel reveals itself as a **tragedy** (see Literary Terms) and we learn the mystery of the 'smash-up' and Ethan's disability.

GLOSSARY

darsn't dare not

tied hand and foot unable to take action

we can fetch it we can hit it, head on

(UNTITLED) EPILOGUE

The epilogue opens with the narrator entering the older Ethan Frome's kitchen. He sees two old women seated around the table in the dim, shabby room. One is tall, bony and graceless. The other is small, grey and crippled. Ethan introduces the narrator to Zeena and Mattie. Next we find the narrator at his lodgings speaking to old Mrs Hale, who opens up to him regarding Ethan's sad story, now that she discovers he has witnessed something of it at first hand. We learn that after the crash, Zeena cared for both Mattie and Ethan, and that Mattie has soured over the years. Mrs Hale also expresses her pity for Ethan and her inability to be in his company as his face is so sad that she cannot bear to look at him. She also expresses her opinion that Ethan would have been better off had Mattie died.

Ironically, *Mattie has become as miserable as Zeena.*

COMMENT

It is **ironic** (see Literary Terms) that Zeena, who was always been determined to be ill, is the one who takes care of Mattie, who was so bright and healthy. Mattie's voice is described as a 'querulous drone' as Zeena's once was. When Ethan comments on how cold the room is, Mattie blames Zeena for having neglected the fire, complaining in a high thin voice. Mattie has become like Zeena.

From Mrs Hale we learn of the community's perception of events at the Frome house. Mrs Hale cannot bring herself to visit when Ethan is around as she is unable to look at his sorrowful face. She perceives, rather eerily, that the only difference between the Fromes in the graveyard and the Fromes at the farm is that the women in the grave have got to hold their tongues.

GLOSSARY

slatternly slovenly, filthy

TEST YOURSELF (CHAPTER 9–EPILOGUE)

A Identify the speaker.

1 'I wanted you should stay and fix up that stove in Mattie's room afore the girl gets here'

2 'Ethan – I thought I wasn't ever going to see you again!'

3 'You were as pretty as a picture in that pink hat!'

4 'I want to do for you and care for you. I want to be there when you're sick and when you're lonesome'

5 'There was one day, about a week after the accident, when they all thought Mattie couldn't live. Well I say it's a pity she *did*'

Identify the person(s) 'to whom' this comment refers.

6 'But she's suffered too much – that's what I always say when folks tell me how she's soured'

7 'When I see that, I think it's *him* that suffers most … anyhow it ain't Zeena, because she ain't got the time'

Check your answers on page 67.

B Consider these issues.

a How the writer creates a sense of **climax** (see Literary Terms) in the closing chapters.

b Why Mattie has become like Zeena.

c How often death is alluded to or spoken of in the novel.

d Your response to the final chapters of this story. Do you think Ethan made the right decision?

e Whether the author has drawn in Ethan a character you can admire and feel sympathy with.

PART THREE

COMMENTARY

THEMES

Themes are the main ideas which run as threads through the text. It is possible to trace how themes are developed by looking at:

- Individual characters and their interactions with each another.
- Events and how they are portrayed.

In this novel, because of the dominance of the major character, Ethan, all the themes are seen through him, his thoughts, feelings, actions, comments and relationships. Principally we are asked to consider the following:

- Longing
- Death and disease
- The effects of the environment
- Money

LONGING

One of the main strands of the novel concerns Ethan's longing. His longing **symbolises** (see Literary Terms) the search for fulfilment in a number of different areas:

- Longing for love (seen in both Ethan's longing for Mattie and in Mattie's longing for Ethan)
- Longing for knowledge and success (Ethan has had to suppress both his desire to continue his education and his desire to work at an interesting job in the city)
- Longing for freedom (Ethan longs to be free of Zeena and to be free of financial constraints)

Longing for love

In Mattie, Ethan has found the possibility of love for the first time in his life. He has found someone with whom he can share the secret part of himself.

Ethan discovers love for the first time.

The two characters share a love and appreciation of nature. Ethan shares what insights into the mysteries of the universe his studies have given him, and Mattie is an appreciative listener. Once, when they stood in awe before a sunset and Mattie said that it looked as though it had been painted, Ethan felt as though she had spoken directly to his soul.

Their longing for one another goes unfulfilled as their situation does not allow them to come together. Ethan spends much of his time secretly longing to be with Mattie. He longs to kiss her, to touch her hand, to spend his days in her company, and to be buried next to her when he dies. It is not until almost the end of the novel when faced with Mattie's leaving that Ethan can speak aloud his feelings for her.

Only when Mattie is about to leave, can Ethan tell her how he feels.

Throughout the novel his longing for her is secret as he struggles with his knowledge that his feelings are inappropriate as he is married to another woman.

Ethan's and Mattie's longing for one another represents the need we all have to be with someone with whom we can share ourselves and with whom we can feel loved and safe.

Longing for knowledge & success

Ethan fails to gain success in his life, because he puts others first.

Ethan's studies were cut short when his parents became ill and he was forced to return to the farm. What knowledge he gained he applied to interpreting nature. He wanted always to become an engineer and to live in a big town where he would be exposed to interesting ideas and people. He desired as well to see the world and felt that with a wife like Zeena this would be possible. However, he soon came to realise the impossibility of Zeena going anywhere.

When Ethan contemplates leaving Zeena, he dreams of taking Mattie 'out West' and finding decent work.

When we first meet the old Ethan Frome, he is interested in a book on biochemistry that the narrator leaves in Ethan's sleigh. It is apparent that the old man still longs for knowledge and is hurt by how he has failed to gain success in his life.

Longing for freedom

Ethan longs to be free of his commitment to his wife. Ethan, when we meet him as a young man, is still full of energy and life, yet Zeena, seven years his senior, in many ways is already an old woman.

Ethan often regrets having asked Zeena to stay and marry him. She is bitter and morbid and does not support and understand him in the way that Mattie does. When Ethan lies next to her at night, he turns away from her and longs to be with Mattie.

Ethan's unhappiness in his marriage reflects the author's own unhappiness.

Ethan's unhappiness in his marriage reflects Edith Wharton's own painful experience of love. She married a man several years older than herself and after twenty-five unhappy years together, they divorced.

DEATH & DISEASE

Death and disease are a major theme of *Ethan Frome*.

Edith Wharton sees disease as part of the human condition, something we are born with or create for ourselves, something real or imaginary that influences how we live our lives. Edith Wharton's own husband suffered from mental illness, and his subsequent nervous collapse precipitated the end of their marriage.

It is difficult to decide whether death is a theme in the novel, or rather a **motif** (see Literary Terms). Death and disease are examined in the novel in several ways.

- Images of death throughout (Ethan lives next to the family graveyard. The idea of death is often present in Ethan's fantasies and in his relationship with his wife.)

- Zeena's hypochondria
- What happens to Ethan and Mattie (rather than separate they wished to die)

Images of death

Early in the story we are told that as a young man Ethan returned to Starkfield to nurse his father who soon died, leaving Ethan in charge of the farm and alone to care for his mother. We learn how she went 'queer' and that she grew silent and eventually died. The family graveyard serves as an ever-present reminder to Ethan that he will never get away, and whenever he passes it by he reflects on the inevitable fact that his life will end at the farm and he will join his relatives in the family graveyard.

Consider the significance of the family graveyard.

Edith Wharton uses many images of death in her descriptions of places. She describes a dead cucumber vine hanging from the porch as being like a streamer tied to the door of a house to denote death. When Mattie and Ethan enter the kitchen late in the evening, the author compares the 'deadly' cold to the chill of a burial chamber.

Zeena haunts Ethan like a ghost.

On several occasions, Ethan sees the face of his wife as if he is seeing a ghost. When Mattie sits in Zeena's chair, it seems to Ethan that the face of his wife obliterates that of Mattie. On their terrifying slide toward the elm tree, Ethan suddenly sees Zeena's face rise up in front of him like a monster, blocking out his goal.

Ethan and Zeena's relationship can be described as being diseased. There is no love between them. Throughout the course of the novel, Ethan loses any fondness for her that he once felt as he comes to blame her for preventing him from making a success of his life. Ethan ceases to believe that Zeena is sick and sees her constant trips to doctors as a way of manipulating him and wasting his money.

Zeena's hypochondria

Zeena is obsessed with the idea that she is riddled with disease. Whenever she appears in a scene, she refers to one of her many pains. The other characters relate to her through her illnesses: as a hypochondriac, she enjoys talking about them. She gains status in the community through her knowledge of disease and the body and exploits every opportunity to elaborate on her own complex set of ailments.

Ethan and Mattie

Ethan and Mattie's decision causes them to live on, crippled, for the rest of their lives.

The state of disease can be a direct result of the choices we make in life. That is certainly the case with Ethan and Mattie. Rather than be parted, they decide, madly, to die together by colliding with the elm tree. The result is that they both spend the rest of their lives struggling with disease. Ethan's face is terribly scarred, and he loses most of the use of his right side. Mattie suffers from a disease of the spine which leaves her unable to walk or move. She also loses her pleasant personality and lust for life, the very qualities Ethan admired in her in the first place.

The effects of the environment

The idea of the environment affecting the development of character is an important theme of *Ethan Frome*, and is explored in three main ways:

- The climate (how the characters are defined and shaped by it)
- The farm (how Ethan feels about it depends upon Zeena's presence or absence)
- Decisions (how the environment affects the decisions people make)

The climate

During the narrator's introduction, he refers often to how the climate has affected the community of Starkfield. When he first arrived he was struck by the disparity between the vitality of the climate and

The silence of the long winter has a depressing effect on the people of Starkfield.

the lifeless community. However, after spending a winter there, he began to understand why the people of Starkfield surrender to the silence of the long winter. When he meets Ethan, it seems to him that Ethan is a part of the silent landscape, representing its 'frozen woe'. Ethan, like the snow-covered land, keeps the warm part of himself well below the surface.

The narrator intuits that Ethan's loneliness is not merely the result of his tragic life, but that it is also the result of having spent too many long cold winters in Starkfield. Harmon Gow hints that everyone who stays in Starkfield is unlucky and says straight out that most of the smart ones escape.

The farm

The kitchen is the main room in Ethan's house. It is the room in which the characters spend most of their time together. It is described as being poor, dark, cold and sparse. When Zeena is at home, Ethan dreads going in there. When Zeena goes to Bettsbridge for the night and Ethan leaves Mattie alone in the kitchen for the afternoon, he reflects on how 'homelike' it feels with Zeena absent. He remarks upon the sun shining in the room while Mattie works and the scene warms his heart.

Decisions

Think how the environment affects the decisions Ethan makes.

In *Ethan Frome* the environment certainly affects the decisions the characters make. When Ethan reflects on his mother's illness, he remembers how he hated her silence. He became so lonely that when Zeena came to nurse his mother, he welcomed the sound of another person's voice. After his mother died, Ethan could not face the thought of spending another long silent winter alone, so he asked Zeena to stay. He was to regret this decision for the rest of his life.

Certainly Ethan and Mattie's rash decision to slide to their deaths would not have been possible had it been spring instead of winter. Perhaps they would have thought things through and have arrived at another solution. Ethan felt the impossibility of going back to that cold house and Zeena, and made a decision that would change all the characters' lives for ever.

MONEY

Money is a major concern of the novel. Through Ethan the author explores the idea that how much money we have defines the choices available to us. This idea is explored in two main ways.

- Money as a cause of conflict (between Ethan and Zeena)
- How lack of money undermines Ethan's attempts to find happiness.

Money as a cause of conflict

Money is often the cause of conflict between Ethan and Zeena. We are told that Ethan has come to dread Zeena's trips to doctors as she always comes home having spent more money than they can afford on remedies and potions. On her last visit to Springfield she paid twenty dollars for an electric battery which she never learned to use.

Poverty causes tensions and restricts independence.

Mattie would never have come to live with the Fromes, had she not been left without money. When Zeena comes home from her trip to Bettsbridge, having hired a girl and offered her a salary without consulting Ethan, they have their first openly angry argument. Zeena blames Mattie for eating up money, calls her a pauper, and accuses her of hanging on to them. This creates even more distance between them as Ethan feels helpless to defend Mattie, lest Zeena suspect his true feelings.

Poverty inhibits choice

Once Ethan is faced with Mattie's leaving, he attempts to find a solution that would benefit them all. When he reflects on the state of his relationship with Zeena,

Think how many times Ethan's plan to leave Zeena is thwarted.

he realises that she is far more bitter and unhappy than when he married her and that her only pleasure left is to cause him pain. He concludes that they would both be better off if they separated. Ethan has the idea of going west with Mattie and beginning a new life. He writes a goodbye note to Zeena and becomes carried away with the idea of being free to love Mattie until he realises he hasn't the money even to travel out west, let alone have something to live on when they get there. He hasn't even the security to borrow ten dollars.

On the day Mattie is to leave, Ethan attempts once again to make real his dream of life with her. He makes his way toward Mr Hale's with the intention of asking for money under the pretext of needing to buy medication for Zeena. On his way he meets Mrs Hale who expresses her sympathy, and Ethan cannot bring himself to lie to these people who have shown him kindness. Ethan is left without a way of obtaining money, and resigns himself to living out his days unhappily, without even the comfort of being near Mattie.

Ethan's fate is determined by his poverty. He has no choice but to stay.

STRUCTURE

The outer story contains an inner story.

Ethan Frome is a short novel. Sometimes these are described as novellas. It is a story told within a frame, or a **frame narrative** (see Literary Terms). The story relates to four days in the life of Ethan Frome that culminate in the event that would determine how he, as well as the other main characters, are to live out their lives.

The frame narrative is contained in the (untitled) introduction and epilogue. The internal narrative (Chapters 1–9) concerns what led to Ethan's 'smash-up', but this story also contains many **flashbacks** (see Literary Terms) to Ethan's life before he knew Mattie.

The structure of *Ethan Frome* is made up of three main sections. The (untitled) introduction, the internal narrative and the (untitled) epilogue.

(Untitled) introduction

The introduction to the story of *Ethan Frome* is told by the narrator in the **first person** (see Literary Terms). We are never told who exactly the narrator is, his name is not given, all we learn is that the narrator is working near Starkfield, and develops an interest in Ethan's life. We meet Ethan first as an elderly middle-aged man, seen through the narrator's eyes. The narrator serves the purpose of setting up the story and stimulating our interest in the character of Ethan Frome and the mystery of his life. We learn that the story we are about to hear is a **tragedy** (see Literary Terms).

Internal narrative

The internal narrative begins twenty-four years before the frame of the novel. It is told in a **third-person narrative** (see Literary Terms). We are introduced to the main characters through scenes that happen in the present tense as well as **flashbacks** (see Literary Terms). The story happens over four days. We know from the beginning that an accident occurred. The story builds toward this inevitable **climax** (see Literary Terms) through circumstances and through relationships.

The FRAME Narrative
INTRODUCTION
THE NARRATOR (undescribed) a stranger to STARKFIELD,
→ MEETS
ETHAN FROME
AND HEARS OF, BUT NEVER SEES, HIS WIFE, ZEENA
ZEENA
CHAPTERS 1 ~ 9
THE NARRATOR DOES NOT INTRUDE ON THE STORY, WHICH TAKES PLACE 24 YEARS EARLIER
ETHAN
ZEENA
MATTIE
EPILOGUE
THE NARRATOR NOW, 24 YEARS LATER, ENTERS ETHAN'S HOME, AND, AT LAST, MEETS THE ELDERLY ZEENA AND CRIPPLED MATTIE

Therefore, even though we have an idea from the very beginning that something tragic has occurred in Ethan's life, we do not know what or how it occurred. Edith Wharton has written a novel about characters and relationships rather than one about suspense.

(Untitled) epilogue

In the epilogue, we meet the narrator once again. He discusses the case with Mrs Hale. She provides us with a perspective of someone involved indirectly with the characters and ends the novel with her bleak assertion that Ethan, Zeena and Mattie are alive without life.

CHARACTERS

We learn about characters through:

- Their own actions and behaviour
- The way they speak and what they are concerned about
- What they think of other characters and incidents
- What other characters think and say about them
- What the writer tells us directly

ETHAN FROME

Ethan is the main character and the story revolves around him. When we first meet Ethan he is described to us by the narrator. He looks old beyond his years, and to the narrator it seems as if Ethan is already dead and buried.

Before we learn much of his personality, we learn of his unusual appearance. He has a deep red scar across his face and a lame right side that makes walking very difficult for him. Despite his shattered body, he gives the impression of being a powerful man.

We learn that Ethan is very poor, and that he has spent his life caring for his ailing family. He is described as

Lame & reticent

Sensitive & intelligent

Honest & passive

A dreamer

being reticent and taciturn, yet not unfriendly. Ethan displays his curiosity when he accepts the narrator's offer to lend him a book on biochemistry. He shows that he can be depended upon when he is determined to drive the narrator through to Corbury Flats and back, even in a storm.

When the internal narrative begins, we meet Ethan as a healthy young man, without any of the physical problems that would bother him later in his life. We learn that Ethan is sensitive and intelligent, and that he has a deep love of nature.

Think why Ethan should feel jealous of Denis Eady.

During the course of the novel we discover some of Ethan's family history, as well his history with Zeena. We learn that Ethan's loneliness and his subsequent fear of being alone led him to propose to Zeena, a decision he would always regret. Yet even though Zeena gives Ethan many reasons for despising her, he always treats her fairly.

Ethan displays his jealousy when he watches Mattie dance with Denis Eady. He admits to himself that he has no right to feel jealous, yet he is helpless to arrest these feelings that are almost violent.

Ethan has a romantic side to his nature which is shown when he fantasises about a life with Mattie. He loves her deeply and dreams of growing old by her side and lying next to her when he dies.

Ethan's kindness is displayed in his treatment of Mattie. To avoid Zeena's complaining of Mattie's poor house skills, Ethan helps whenever he can, sometimes getting up early to clean the floors.

Ethan is an honest man. Even when he is desperate and has decided to lie to Mr Hale to obtain an advance of money for his planned flight with Mattie, he cannot go through with it. He will not take advantage of other people.

Ethan is a rather inarticulate person. He does not often engage in dialogue, and when he does he says as little as possible. He cannot express his feelings in words. One of the many examples of this is, when walking Mattie home – he tries to come up with something dazzling to say and all he can think of is to tell her to 'come along'.

Perhaps Ethan's flaw is that he is too passive. He stands back and allows the women in his life to make crucial decisions for him. He does not stand up to Zeena when, much to his despair, she insists that Mattie must leave. He is easily defeated by his wife and allows her to make decisions that lead to his unhappiness. Ethan goes along with Mattie's idea of tobogganing into the elm tree, with disastrous consequences. He allows himself to be easily swayed by others and cannot fight for what he wants. Even though we may feel frustration for Ethan's passivity, we do feel sympathy for him and he is essentially a very likeable character.

ZEENA

Sickly & complaining
Manipulative & petty
Spendthrift & self-indulgent

Zeena is Ethan's wife and cousin, an unpleasant woman who is the cause of much of Ethan's unhappiness. She is described as being sickly, drawn and bloodless, and having a face with 'querulous lines', and 'lashless lids'. Though she is only thirty-five, she seems to be an old woman.

Zeena's most obvious characteristic is her hypochondria. She is obsessed with herself and her apparently ailing body. In every scene in which she appears in the novel, she refers to her health. She complains of feeling so 'mean' that she is unable to sleep, of having unbearable shooting pains, of not being able to go on as the pain has reached all the way to her ankles. She claims that the doctor does not think she should do any work around the house, and demands that Ethan hire a girl to take care of her.

During the course of the novel, Ethan ceases to believe that Zeena is really sick. He realises that his wife is manipulating him into getting rid of Mattie and spending money he does not have on hiring someone else.

Zeena is petty, seeking to find fault with Mattie however she can. Her fault-finding is of the silent kind and Ethan fears how her disfavour will manifest itself.

Even the sound of Zeena's voice is unpleasant, described as a flat whine.

Zeena does not treat Ethan with the respect he has always shown her.

Zeena is a spendthrift, wasting Ethan's money on various medicines and potions that never seem to have much effect. Once she paid twenty dollars for an electric battery which she never learned to use.

Ethan comes to blame Zeena's narrow-mindedness and ignorance for his failure to make a success of his life. He feels that he has sacrificed all his possibilities for this miserable woman whose sole remaining pleasure is to cause him pain.

Zeena's **dialect** (see Literary Terms) betrays her lack of education. 'You ain't got the money?' (p. 85) she demands of Ethan after she's hired a girl. 'Dan'l Byrne says he darsn't leave that horse' (p. 106) she offers as an excuse for there being no help with Mattie's trunk. Edith Wharton has given Zeena a way of speaking that is unlike any of the other characters.

At the end of the novel we learn that, despite her supposed illnesses, Zeena has found the strength to look after Mattie, and manage the house on her own. This is perhaps her only redeeming quality. In Zeena, Edith Wharton has created a character whom we are unable to sympathise with.

MATTIE

Pleasant & young
Appreciative & sensitive
Impulsive

Mattie is Zeena's cousin and comes to live with Ethan and Zeena after the death of her father. When Ethan reflects on meeting Mattie for the first time, he remembers how thin and pale she was on the day she came to Starkfield. Ethan had been afraid that Mattie would hate life in cold and lonely Starkfield, yet she never once complained.

Mattie is a very pleasant character, full of youth and life – she enjoys laughing and dancing. She has improved Ethan's existence immensely since coming to Starkfield and is able to appreciate him in a way nobody else does.

She is sensitive and shares with Ethan a love of nature. She is a willing audience for Ethan's attempts to explain the mysteries of the world and listens in a way that infuses him with confidence.

Mattie displays strength of character when, after discovering that Zeena has decided she is to leave, she does not cry or complain, but rather seeks to comfort Ethan.

Mattie is an impulsive character, and in a rash moment convinces Ethan of committing suicide with her. Mattie's inability to deal with taking care of herself would cause her to act in such a way that could only end in disaster.

When we meet Mattie at the end of the novel, she is a withered old cripple. Her voice is a 'querulous drone', as she sits in the kitchen complaining of the cold. The general perception is that Mattie has soured. Gone is the pleasant girl; in her place is a woman who behaves much in the way that Zeena did.

MINOR CHARACTERS

The narrator We are not given a name or a physical description of the narrator. We can discern that he is a man, and that he has been sent to Massachusetts by his employers on a job to do with the electricity plant at Corbury Flats. He rents a room in Mrs Ned Hale's house and becomes curious to find out more about Ethan Frome. He appears to be a sensitive and thoughtful person, who tries to engage Ethan in conversation.

Harmon Gow

Harmon Gow is a local man who used to drive the stagecoach from Bettsbridge to Starkfield and is familiar with the histories of all the families in the area. It is he who tells the narrator a little about Ethan, at least as far as he is able. The narrator refers to him as the local 'oracle', and it is Harmon who suggests that the narrator hire Ethan to drive him to his work in Corbury Flats.

Denis Eady

Denis is the dark, handsome son of Michael Eady, an ambitious Irish grocer. Denis works in his father's business. He attempts to woo Mattie.

He is a source of Ethan's troubles, for he becomes jealous of Denis's looks, youthfulness and prosperity and his obvious suitability as a potential husband for Mattie, since he is unattached and likely to inherit his father's thriving business. However, Mattie may flirt with him, but she has no serious feelings about him.

Denis seems to be everything that Ethan is not. He is outgoing, friendly, robust and very likely to be successful. He seems to be free of the worries and troubles that make Ethan so grave.

The Hale family

Andrew Hale is a builder to whom Ethan sells his lumber. He has a large family and, though his business does well, he is known to overspend. He is an old friend of Ethan's family, and a kind man. Andrew's wife is a kind woman who expresses her sympathy for Ethan. Ned their son is engaged to Ruth Varnum.

Ruth Varnum Ruth is a friend of Mattie's. We meet her in the **frame narrative** (see Literary Terms) as Mrs Hale. She is a widow with whom the narrator lodges. She provides us with the perspective of someone indirectly involved with the tragedy of Ethan Frome.

Jotham Powell Jotham is a local man who occasionally works for Ethan. He is a rather inarticulate person.

Daniel Byrne Daniel is a local man whom Zeena has engaged to take Mattie's trunk to the train station.

LANGUAGE & STYLE

There are two separate styles in *Ethan Frome* . One is descriptive and often poetic, the other simple and **colloquial** (see Literary Terms). It is a testament to Edith Wharton's talent that she is able to blend these two styles together with such effect.

DESCRIPTIVE STYLE

Think of other examples of Edith Wharton's metaphors and similes.

This owes its success to Edith Wharton's eye for minute observation of nature and her gift for unusual and evocative **metaphors** and **similes** (see Literary Terms). As one example, she describes outcrops of slate that jut out of the snow as being 'like animals pushing out their noses to breathe' (p. 15). At first reading this simile may seem rather strange. Preceding the simile is a description of starved-looking apple trees trying desperately to thrive between the stones. The **image** (see Literary Terms) is startling and we begin to develop a picture in our minds of a rough landscape where fruit does not easily grow, where nature, like the people, must struggle to survive. It is a land that does not lend itself easily to life, so that, like the animals forcing through the snow to breathe, people like Ethan must struggle to eke out a living.

Edith Wharton's powerful descriptive style gives the reader a vivid sense of place. She describes the farmhouses that exist here and there in the fields as being 'mute and cold as a gravestone' (p. 37). This image is so evocative that we immediately have a sense and a picture of the place she describes.

Edith Wharton's use of light

Edith Wharton often uses light in her descriptive passages. She uses it to expose ugliness: 'a flash of watery sunlight exposed the house on the slope above us in all its plaintive ugliness' (p. 15). She also uses it to illuminate beauty: 'She held the light at the same level … Then, striking upward, it threw a lustrous fleck on her lips, edged her eyes with velvet shade, and laid a milky whiteness above the black curve of her brows' (p. 60).

COLLOQUIAL LANGUAGE

Edith Wharton makes rather heavy use of **dialogue** (see Literary Terms), and recreates directly the vernacular and **colloquial** (see Literary Terms) language of the rural New Englanders. She writes as they speak, and recreates their language with unfaltering accuracy. In doing so, she uses language that is often grammatically incorrect, yet it is vivid, alive and indicative of the character's lack of education.

Most of the characters struggle with expressing themselves in words and, especially Ethan, avoid speaking unless absolutely necessary. The result is that in Ethan's case he speaks in short direct sentences.

In Zeena's case, the grammatical errors and vernacular language are more pronounced. 'I wanted you should stay and fix up that stove in Mattie's room afore the girl gets here. It ain't been drawing right for nigh on a month now' (p. 109).

The way Edith Wharton writes dialogue tells us a lot about the characters. The blending of these two aspects of her writing – her use of colloquial language and her descriptive style – is one of the reasons why *Ethan Frome* is such a remarkable novel.

PART FOUR

STUDY SKILLS

HOW TO USE QUOTATIONS

One of the secrets of success in writing essays is the way you use quotations. There are five basic principles:

- Put inverted commas at the beginning and end of the quotation
- Write the quotation exactly as it appears in the original
- Do not use a quotation that repeats what you have just written
- Use the quotation so that it fits into your sentence
- Keep the quotation as short as possible

Quotations should be used to develop the line of thought in your essays.

Your comment should not duplicate what is in your quotation. For example:

> **Zeena openly reveals her suspicion of Ethan's romantic feelings for Mattie only once. Ethan warns her that if she forces Mattie to leave folks will talk, and Zeena's response is this, 'I know well enough what they say of my having kep' her here as long as I have' (p. 87).**

Far more effective is to write:

> **We learn that Zeena suspects what is between Ethan and Mattie when she says, 'I know well enough what they say of my having kep' her here as long as I have' (p. 87).**

However, the most sophisticated way of using the writer's words is to embed them into your sentence:

> **When Zeena says, 'I know well enough what they say of my having kep' her here as long as I have,' she reveals her suspicion of Ethan's love of Mattie (p. 87).**

When you use quotations in this way, you are demonstrating the ability to use text as evidence to support your ideas - not simply including words from the original to prove you have read it.

Everyone writes differently. Work through the suggestions given here and adapt the advice to suit your own style and interests. This will improve your essay-writing skills and allow your personal voice to emerge.

The following points indicate in ascending order the skills of essay writing:

- Picking out one or two facts about the story and adding the odd detail
- Writing about the text by retelling the story
- Retelling the story and adding a quotation here and there
- Organising an answer which explains what is happening in the text and giving quotations to support what you write

....

- Writing in such a way as to show that you have thought about the intentions of the writer of the text and that you understand the techniques used
- Writing at some length, giving your viewpoint on the text and commenting by picking out details to support your views
- Looking at the text as a work of art, demonstrating clear critical judgement and explaining to the reader of your essay how the enjoyment of the text is assisted by literary devices, linguistic effects and psychological insights; showing how the text relates to the time when it was written

The dotted line above represents the division between lower- and higher-level grades. Higher-level performance begins when you start to consider your response as a reader of the text. The highest level is reached when you offer an enthusiastic personal response and show how this piece of literature is a product of its time.

Coursework essay

Set aside an hour or so at the start of your work to plan what you have to do.

- List all the points you feel are needed to cover the task. Collect page references of information and quotations that will support what you have to say. A helpful tool is the highlighter pen: this saves painstaking copying and enables you to target precisely what you want to use.
- Focus on what you consider to be the main points of the essay. Try to sum up your argument in a single sentence, which could be the closing sentence of your essay. Depending on the essay title, it could be a statement about a character: Zeena is the character responsible for Ethan's unhappiness, because she is so wrapped up in herself that she never shows him any love and understanding: she only shows him contempt; an opinion about a setting:The cold and bleakness of Starkfield reflects the lifeless and defeated nature of the characters; or a judgement on a theme: One of the central themes in *Ethan Frome* is longing, as Ethan spends a great deal of his time longing for things that will bring him happiness.
- Make a short essay plan. Use the first paragraph to introduce the argument you wish to make. In the following paragraphs develop this argument with details, examples and other possible points of view. Sum up your argument in the last paragraph. Check you have answered the question.
- Write the essay, remembering all the time the central point you are making.
- On completion, go back over what you have written to eliminate careless errors and improve expression. Read it aloud to yourself, or, if you are feeling more confident, to a relative or friend.

If you can, try to type your essay, using a word processor. This will allow you to correct and improve your writing without spoiling its appearance.

Examination essay

The essay written in an examination often carries more marks than the coursework essay even though it is written under considerable time pressure.

In the revision period build up notes on various aspects of the text you are using. Fortunately, in acquiring this set of York Notes on *Ethan Frome*, you have made a prudent beginning! York Notes are set out to give you vital information and help you to construct your personal overview of the text.

Make notes with appropriate quotations about the key issues of the set text. Go into the examination knowing your text and having a clear set of opinions about it.

In most English Literature examinations you can take in copies of your set books. This in an enormous advantage although it may lull you into a false sense of security. Beware! There is simply not enough time in an examination to read the book from scratch.

In the examination

- Read the question paper carefully and remind yourself what you have to do.
- Look at the questions on your set texts to select the one that most interests you and mentally work out the points you wish to stress.
- Remind yourself of the time available and how you are going to use it.
- Briefly map out a short plan in note form that will keep your writing on track and illustrate the key argument you want to make.
- Then set about writing it.
- When you have finished, check through to eliminate errors.

To summarise, these are the keys to success:

- **Know the text**
- **Have a clear understanding of and opinions on the storyline, characters, setting, themes and writer's concerns**
- **Select the right material**
- **Plan and write a clear response, continually bearing the question in mind**

A typical essay question on *Ethan Frome* is followed by a sample essay plan in note form. This does not present the only answer to the question, merely one answer. Do not be afraid to include your own ideas and disregard some of those in the sample. Remember that quotations are essential to prove and illustrate the points you make.

To what extent is *Ethan Frome* a novel about the human need for love and understanding, and the desperate lengths people will go to in order to achieve it?

Introduction

The main theme and plot of Edith Wharton's tragic novel, *Ethan Frome*, is formed around the human need for love and understanding and the desperate lengths people will go to in order to achieve it.

Part One

The characters are willing to make sacrifices to gain the love and respect of others.

- Ethan sacrifices his education and career potential to return to Starkfield to care for his ailing parents
- Zeena sacrifices her time and energy to nurse Ethan's mother
- Mattie slaves for Zeena and Ethan to remain in their home

Part Two

The need for love and understanding affects the characters' behaviour.

- Zeena's hypochondria is her way of getting attention
- Ethan helps Mattie with her chores, neglecting his own work
- Ethan lies to Zeena so that he may spend time with Mattie

Part Three

The need for love and understanding causes the characters to make rash decisions.

- Ethan asking Zeena to marry him
- Ethan deciding to run away with Mattie
- Mattie and Ethan deciding to commit suicide together

SAMPLE ESSAY PLAN continued

Conclusion Edith Wharton's novel *Ethan Frome* shows that humans have such a desperate need to be loved and understood that they will go to any lengths to fulfil that need, even to the extent that they are willing to die for it.

FURTHER QUESTIONS

1. Are there any weaknesses in *Ethan Frome* ?
2. How significant is the theme of longing in *Ethan Frome* ?
3. Why does Ethan not abandon Zeena?
4. Does Edith Wharton sympathise with Zeena, or does she condemn her?
5. What are the main techniques that Edith Wharton uses to create atmosphere in *Ethan Frome* ?
6. Select three scenes which you think are vital to the novel and explain your choice.
7. Explain how each of the three major characters of the novel, Ethan, Mattie and Zeena, is important to our understanding of what the novel is about?

PART FIVE

CULTURAL CONNECTIONS

BROADER PERSPECTIVES

Anyone studying *Ethan Frome* should also read what is usually thought of as Edith Wharton's masterpiece, *The Age of Innocence* (1920). It is very different from *Ethan Frome* , but noting the differences can reveal the strengths (and perhaps the weaknesses) of the two novels. The novel deals with New York Society and manners, and is thought of as Edith Wharton's most skilfully constructed work. It was awarded the Pulitzer Prize for fiction in 1921, making Edith Wharton the first woman ever to achieve that distinction.

Some of her other novels that deal with New York society are: *The House of Mirth* (1905), which chronicles the life of a failed social climber Lily Bart, and *The Custom of the Country* (1913), which describes the breakdown of traditional New York culture.

A film version of *Ethan Frome* was made in 1993 and starred Liam Neeson, Patricia Arquette and Joan Allen. It is directed by Richard Pryce and is an American Playhouse production. It is seen as a well-acted production, yet also as a little dry.

A modern film version of *The Age of Innocence* was made in 1993 by Columbia Pictures. It stars Daniel Day-Lewis, Michelle Pfeiffer and Winona Ryder. It received mixed reviews, but is worth seeing.

Henry James was both a friend and a mentor to Edith Wharton. Anyone familiar with his work will notice his influence on Edith Wharton's writing. His most famous works are: *The Portrait of a Lady* (1881), and *The Wings of the Dove* (1902). Both novels have recently been made into films. *The Portrait of a Lady* was made in 1996, and stars Nicole Kidman and John Malkovitch.

It is beautifully filmed and is an above-average production. *The Wings of the Dove* was made in 1997 and stars Helena Bonham Carter and Linus Roach. It is a stunning film for which Ms Bonham Carter was nominated for an Oscar.

There are a number of good biographies of Edith Wharton. Anyone who wishes to learn more about her can begin with *Edith Wharton, a Biography* by R.W.B. Lewis (Constable, 1975). *Edith Wharton; a study of her fiction* by Blake Nevius (University of California Press/ Cambridge University Press, 1953) is also good. They both provide a fascinating insight into the mind and life of a great writer and a great woman.

CHRONOLOGY

Year	World Events	Year	Author's Life	Literary Events	Year
1775-83	Thirteen American colonies win independence from Britain	1775	Ebenezer Stevens, Edith's grandfather, a general in the Revolutionary War		
1860	Abraham Lincoln becomes President of the USA			Charles Dickens, *Great Expectations*	1860-1
1861	American Civil War begins				
		1862	Edith Newbold Jones born into wealthy Stevens Jones family, New York		
1863	Abolition of slavery proclaimed in USA				
1865	Civil War ends; Lincoln assassinated				
				Elizabeth Gaskell, *Wives and Daughters*	1866
		1867	Edith educated at home		
				Charles Dickens dies	1870
				George Eliot, *Middlemarch*	1871
				Thomas Hardy, *Under the Greenwood Tree*	1872
1873	First commercially successful typewriter				
1874	First Impressionist exhibition in Paris				
1875	Baked beans canned for the first time				
				Henry James, *The Americans*	1876

WORLD EVENTS	AUTHOR'S LIFE	LITERARY EVENTS
1879 First cash register, fridge, milk bottle, electric streetcar	1879 Edith joins the New York social scene	
1880 First successful inoculations		
1881 First tricycle lawnmower, electric railway		
		Guy de Maupassant, 'Country Living', one of his many short stories about poor rural life 1883
1884 First rollercoaster, Coney Island		
1885 First petrol-driven car	1885 Edith marries Edward Wharton, 12 years her senior	
1886 First successful electric street lighting invented by George Westinghouse		Emile Zola, *La Terre* (Earth) 1886
1888 First pneumatic tyre		
	1889 Edith's sonnet 'Happiness' published in *Scribner's Magazine*	
1890 First aeroplane flies for 50 metres		
		Thomas Hardy, *Tess of the D'Urbervilles* 1891
	1897 Edith begins writing fiction	
		H.G. Wells, *The War of the Worlds* 1898
	1899 Publishes first short stories, *The Greater Inclination*	
	1900 First novella, *The Touchstone*	

Chronology

World Events		Author's Life		Literary Events	
1901	Beginning of 'Edwardian Era' that will last until outbreak of First World War; trolley-bus tracks being laid at Lenox	1901	Builds country estate at Lenox, Berkshire County Massachusetts; a neighbour to Westinghouse		
1902	Hormones first discovered	1902	Publishes first novel *The Valley of Decision*		
1904	First slow-motion film	1904	*Berkshire Evening Eagle* reports 'coasting' accident: 'Lenox High School Girl Dashed to Her Death': a source for *Ethan Frome*		
1905	Einstein's Theory of Relativity	1905	*The House of Mirth*		
1907	First detergent, electric vacuum cleaner	1907	Moves to France		
		1911	***Ethan Frome***	Katherine Mansfield, *In a German Pension*	1911
1913	Niels Bohr develops Quantum Theory	1913	Edith and Edward divorce; *The Custom of the Country*		
1914-18	First World War	1914	Edith does extensive humanitarian work		
				Willa Cather, *My Antonia*	1918
		1920	*The Age of Innocence*		
		1921	Awarded Pulitzer Prize		
				D.H.Lawrence, *The Plumed Serpent*	1926
		1934	*A Backward Glance* autobiography		
		1937	Dies, having written over 40 books		

LITERARY TERMS

atmosphere the prevailing tone or mood of a novel, symphony, painting, etc.

climax a decisive moment in a dramatic or other work

colloquial ordinary or familiar conversation

dialogue the speech and conversation of characters in a novel, play, or poem. Capturing the 'feel' of real speech is one of the hardest things a novelist has to do

epilogue a short conclusion to any literary work

first-person narrative a story told in the first-person singular (by an 'I' figure who is directly involved)

flashback a sudden jump backwards in time to an earlier episode, giving the reader a fuller picture as the past is described as well as the present

foreshadow to indicate, hint, or suggest what will occur later in the plot of a literary or filmic work

frame narrative the outer, containing story, which is a pretext for the more significant narrative embedded within it

images something described by the writer to create a particular mental impression in the reader

irony incongruity between what is expected to be and what actually is, or a situation or result showing such incongruity

metaphor a comparison in which it is stated that something 'is' another thing rather than that it resembles it

motif an idea or theme which recurs throughout the text

realism style of writing that seeks to represent the familiar or typical in real life

symbol a simple idea or object which is used to convey a more complicated idea

theme central idea or ideas that are examined with a view to some serious questions being asked, and some conclusions being drawn; the overriding topic or topics that interest a writer in his or her book. Longing is a theme in *Ethan Frome*

third-person narrative a way of telling a story about people who are described in the third person (he, she, they) by a narrator who does not write as 'I' but as an unseen observer of events

tragedy any dramatic or literary composition dealing with serious or sombre themes and ending with disaster

TEST ANSWERS

Test yourself (Untitled) introduction–Chapter 2)

A
1 Harmon Gow
2 Narrator
3 Zeena
4 Denis Eady
5 Ethan
6 Ethan
7 Mattie
8 Zeena

Test yourself (Chapters 3–5)

A
1 Zeena
2 Mr Hale
3 Ethan
4 Mattie
5 Ethan
6 Jotham Powell
7 Zeena
8 Ned Hale and Ruth Varnum

Test yourself (Chapters 6–8)

A
1 Denis Eady
2 Jotham Powell
3 Zeena
4 Ethan
5 Mrs Hale
6 Mattie
7 Mr Hale
8 Zeena and Dr Buck

Test yourself (Chapters 9–(Untitled) epilogue)

A
1 Zeena
2 Mattie
3 Ethan
4 Ethan
5 Mrs Hale
6 Mattie
7 Ethan

GCSE and equivalent levels (£3.50 each)

Maya Angelou
I Know Why the Caged Bird Sings

Jane Austen
Pride and Prejudice

Alan Ayckbourn
Absent Friends

Elizabeth Barrett Browning
Selected Poems

Robert Bolt
A Man for All Seasons

Harold Brighouse
Hobson's Choice

Charlotte Brontë
Jane Eyre

Emily Brontë
Wuthering Heights

Shelagh Delaney
A Taste of Honey

Charles Dickens
David Copperfield

Charles Dickens
Great Expectations

Charles Dickens
Hard Times

Charles Dickens
Oliver Twist

Roddy Doyle
Paddy Clarke Ha Ha Ha

George Eliot
Silas Marner

George Eliot
The Mill on the Floss

William Golding
Lord of the Flies

Oliver Goldsmith
She Stoops To Conquer

Willis Hall
The Long and the Short and the Tall

Thomas Hardy
Far from the Madding Crowd

Thomas Hardy
The Mayor of Casterbridge

Thomas Hardy
Tess of the d'Urbervilles

Thomas Hardy
The Withered Arm and other Wessex Tales

L.P. Hartley
The Go-Between

Seamus Heaney
Selected Poems

Susan Hill
I'm the King of the Castle

Barry Hines
A Kestrel for a Knave

Louise Lawrence
Children of the Dust

Harper Lee
To Kill a Mockingbird

Laurie Lee
Cider with Rosie

Arthur Miller
The Crucible

Arthur Miller
A View from the Bridge

Robert O'Brien
Z for Zachariah

Frank O'Connor
My Oedipus Complex and Other Stories

George Orwell
Animal Farm

J.B. Priestley
An Inspector Calls

Willy Russell
Educating Rita

Willy Russell
Our Day Out

J.D. Salinger
The Catcher in the Rye

William Shakespeare
Henry IV Part 1

William Shakespeare
Henry V

William Shakespeare
Julius Caesar

William Shakespeare
Macbeth

William Shakespeare
The Merchant of Venice

William Shakespeare
A Midsummer Night's Dream

William Shakespeare
Much Ado About Nothing

William Shakespeare
Romeo and Juliet

William Shakespeare
The Tempest

William Shakespeare
Twelfth Night

George Bernard Shaw
Pygmalion

Mary Shelley
Frankenstein

R.C. Sherriff
Journey's End

Rukshana Smith
Salt on the Snow

John Steinbeck
Of Mice and Men

Robert Louis Stevenson
Dr Jekyll and Mr Hyde

Jonathan Swift
Gulliver's Travels

Robert Swindells
Daz 4 Zoe

Mildred D. Taylor
Roll of Thunder, Hear My Cry

Mark Twain
Huckleberry Finn

James Watson
Talking in Whispers

William Wordsworth
Selected Poems

A Choice of Poets

Mystery Stories of the Nineteenth Century including The Signalman

Nineteenth Century Short Stories

Poetry of the First World War

Six Women Poets

York Notes Advanced (£3.99 each)

Margaret Atwood
Cat's Eye

Margaret Atwood
The Handmaid's Tale

Jane Austen
Mansfield Park

Jane Austen
Persuasion

Jane Austen
Pride and Prejudice

Alan Bennett
Talking Heads

William Blake
Songs of Innocence and of Experience

Charlotte Brontë
Jane Eyre

Emily Brontë
Wuthering Heights

Angela Carter
Nights at the Circus

Geoffrey Chaucer
The Franklin's Prologue and Tale

Geoffrey Chaucer
The Miller's Prologue and Tale

Geoffrey Chaucer
Prologue To the Canterbury Tales

Geoffrey Chaucer
The Wife of Bath's Prologue and Tale

Samuel Taylor Coleridge
Selected Poems

Joseph Conrad
Heart of Darkness

Daniel Defoe
Moll Flanders

Charles Dickens
Great Expectations

Charles Dickens
Hard Times

Emily Dickinson
Selected Poems

John Donne
Selected Poems

Carol Ann Duffy
Selected Poems

George Eliot
Middlemarch

George Eliot
The Mill on the Floss

T.S. Eliot
Selected Poems

F. Scott Fitzgerald
The Great Gatsby

E.M. Forster
A Passage to India

Brian Friel
Translations

Thomas Hardy
The Mayor of Casterbridge

Thomas Hardy
The Return of the Native

Thomas Hardy
Selected Poems

Thomas Hardy
Tess of the d'Urbervilles

Seamus Heaney
Selected Poems from Opened Ground

Nathaniel Hawthorne
The Scarlet Letter

Kazuo Ishiguro
The Remains of the Day

Ben Jonson
The Alchemist

James Joyce
Dubliners

John Keats
Selected Poems

Christopher Marlowe
Doctor Faustus

Arthur Miller
Death of a Salesman

John Milton
Paradise Lost Books I & II

Toni Morrison
Beloved

Alexander Pope
Rape of the Lock and other poems

William Shakespeare
Antony and Cleopatra

William Shakespeare
As You Like It

William Shakespeare
Hamlet

William Shakespeare
King Lear

William Shakespeare
Measure for Measure

William Shakespeare
The Merchant of Venice

William Shakespeare
A Midsummer Night's Dream

William Shakespeare
Much Ado About Nothing

William Shakespeare
Othello

William Shakespeare
Richard II

William Shakespeare
Romeo and Juliet

William Shakespeare
The Taming of the Shrew

William Shakespeare
The Tempest

William Shakespeare
The Winter's Tale

George Bernard Shaw
Saint Joan

Mary Shelley
Frankenstein

Alice Walker
The Color Purple

Oscar Wilde
The Importance of Being Earnest

Tennessee Williams
A Streetcar Named Desire

John Webster
The Duchess of Malfi

Virginia Woolf
To the Lighthouse

W.B. Yeats
Selected Poems

FUTURE TITLES IN THE YORK NOTES SERIES

Chinua Achebe
Things Fall Apart

Jane Austen
Emma

Jane Austen
Northanger Abbey

Jane Austen
Sense and Sensibility

Samuel Beckett
Waiting for Godot and *Endgame*

Louis de Bernières
Captain Corelli's Mandolin

Charlotte Brontë
Villette

Geoffrey Chaucer
The Merchant's Tale

Geoffrey Chaucer
The Nun's Priest's Tale

Caryl Churchill
Top Girls and *Cloud Nine*

Charles Dickens
Bleak House

T.S. Eliot
The Waste Land

Henry Fielding
Joseph Andrews

Anne Frank
The Diary of Anne Frank

Thomas Hardy
Jude the Obscure

Homer
The Iliad

Homer
The Odyssey

Henrik Ibsen
The Doll's House and *Ghosts*

Ben Jonson
Volpone

James Joyce
A Portrait of the Artist as a Young Man

Philip Larkin
Selected Poems

Aldous Huxley
Brave New World

D.H. Lawrence
Selected Poems

Christopher Marlowe
Edward II

John Milton
Paradise Lost Bks IV & IX

Thomas More
Utopia

George Orwell
Nineteen Eighty-four

Sylvia Plath
Selected Poems

J.B. Priestley
When We Are Married

Jean Rhys
Wide Sargasso Sea

William Shakespeare
As You Like It

William Shakespeare
Coriolanus

William Shakespeare
Henry IV Pt I

Wliiam Shakespeare
Henry IV Part II

William Shakespeare
Henry V

William Shakespeare
Julius Caesar

William Shakespeare
Macbeth

William Shakespeare
Richard III

William Shakespeare
Sonnets

William Shakespeare
Twelfth Night

Tom Stoppard
Arcadia and *Rosencrantz and Guildenstern are Dead*

Jonathan Swift
Gulliver's Travels and A Modest Proposal

Alfred, Lord Tennyson
Selected Poems

Virgil
The Aeneid

Edith Wharton
Ethan Frome

Jeanette Winterson
Oranges are Not the Only Fruit

Tennessee Williams
Cat on a Hot Tin Roof

Virginia Woolf
Mrs Dalloway

Metaphysical Poets

NOTES

NOTES